Grandma Mary

Says Things Happen:

A guide to help children who have experienced trauma

By Gladys Noll Alvarez, LISW & Dustin Daugherty, LISW

Illustrations by Marcia Bradley, MA

xulon PRESS

Grandma Mary Says Things Happen:
A guide to help children who have experienced trauma

by Gladys Noll Alvarez, LISW & Dustin Daugherty, LISW

Printed in the United States of America

Edited by Xulon Press

ISBN 9781498437547

www.xulonpress.com

Dear Parent or Guardian,

       e want this book to be helpful to you and your child to understand trauma. Trauma is something that happens that threatens our sense of safety, either physically or psychologically. Traumatization happens when our internal/external resources are not sufficient to help us cope. Internal resources are things that people can't see that occur on the inside, such as temperament, mood, self-esteem, cognitive skills, perceptions, and/or outlooks. External resources are things such as family support, physical environment, family income, and social support networks (i.e. churches, friends, or teachers). Here are some things that you can do to help your child feel stronger. First, the most important thing is to listen to your child, with the understanding that it is not easy for him/her to communicate how he/she is feeling. This could require a lot of patience. Let your child know that all feelings are ok and legitimate. It is also important to help them learn healthy ways to handle stress, such as deep breathing, coloring, listening to music, taking a walk, or swinging. There are many resources that can be used, several of which are on the following websites: www.resiliencetrumpsaces.org or http://traumainformedcareproject.org/resources.php. Lastly, it is important to let your child know which adults are safe, such as a teacher, a counselor, or a police officer; and give your child permission to talk with safe adults.

To our families and those who have taught us the meaning of resilience and the importance of relationships.

i, I am known as Grandma Mary. This is a nickname people in Cottage Grove give me, because I act like a grandma. I used to be a kindergarten teacher. I love taking care of and helping people, kids in particular.

I am known for my wonderful chocolate chip cookies and the rocking chair on my front porch. I have a really cool sandbox and a tree with a tire swing. Kids come to my yard to play or talk.

There are many kinds of people in Cottage Grove, but one thing I have found is that many of them have had bad things happen to them. Can you tell which kids have had something bad happen to them just by looking? Most people cannot tell the difference just by looking at them.

Some people call these bad things *trauma*. Do you know what trauma is? Even if you do, I bet there are some things that you are not sure about. Here is what I know about trauma.

Trauma is something that happens to make us feel over-whelmed, like a car accident or someone dying. We may feel like we don't know what to do, where to go, how to act, or what to say.

Many kinds of "bad things" (trauma) can happen to a kid or families. They can leave us feeling sad, scared, mad, hyper, on guard, different from others, or just numb with no feelings at all.

And I want to clear something up right now! Some people think that bad things only happen to bad people. That is not true at all!

Traumatic things can happen to anyone, anywhere, at any age. Let me tell you about some kids I know.

James, who is seven and in first grade, lives with my friends from church because he can't live with his mom and dad. He is very smart and funny. He can always make a person laugh and loves helping his teacher during cleanup time.

There is Isabella who is ten years old and in fifth grade. She comes to my house because she gets scared when her parents fight. She is very easy to get along with and a real go-getter. She wants to be a pilot when she grows up. She is really smart and always seems to know the answer when someone asks her a question. So you see, just because they had a trauma, doesn't mean they can't have fun, help others, or live happy lives.

The thing about trauma is that not everyone will respond the same when it happens. It can make a person act differently than what others would expect because of all the confusing feelings that come from trauma. Sometimes this can happen even a long time after the event (trauma).

I know another girl, Sierra. She is eight years old and was abused by her uncle when she was three. Sometimes she will freeze up like a statue when her teacher's voice needs to be loud to give directions. This is how it really is.

The loud noise reminds her of what happened with her uncle. Even though she is safe, Sierra doesn't feel safe. This is how the teacher's voice feels to Sierra.

Sometimes things remind people of trauma. It can be a smell, a touch, a sound, a taste, or seeing something that brings back all those confusing feelings. It might be hard to sit still or pay attention. The reminders are called triggers.

Sometimes it can be really hard to figure out that these feelings and behaviors are about the past and not what is going on now. This makes it even harder to explain to adults what is going on. Adults sometimes have a hard time understanding that the child's feelings are real and can be scary.

One thing that I know for sure is that even if it's really hard to explain or understand, it's never the kid's fault!

There are things kids can do and people who can help. By talking to parents, counselors, teachers, friends, and/or trusted adults, kids can figure out how to feel safe again.

Let me share some of the things the kids told me they do that helps. Whenever James gets sad because he can't live with his mom and dad, he thinks about his grandpa's farm because it makes him feel safe and loved. He remembers the smell of his grandma's homemade bread and playing outside with his cousins. Remembering a happy time could help you or a friend with trauma.

When Sierra gets scared, she remembers to breathe deeply by pretending to smell flowers and blow out birthday candles. She does this really slowly, and it helps her to feel safe again.

Sierra remembers what her mom told her to do when she gets scared so she can keep moving when she feels like freezing. She plays a game where she pretends to be either Raggedy Ann or a robot. The game helps her to relax her tense muscles and calms her down.

There are lots of things that can help with the confusing feelings like drawing or listening to music.

Some other things that can help are swinging, exercising, or just talking to somebody.

Remember, trauma is something that happens to make us feel like we don't know what to do, where to go, how to act, or what to say.

If this happens to you, do what James, Isabella, and Sierra did and talk with an adult who can help. Keep talking until someone does help, and remember that there is always something you can do!

CPSIA information can be obtained
at www.ICGtesting.com
Printed in the USA
BVHW022152150320
574848BV00008B/133